I'm a New Creation... Now What?

LYNDLE SAVAGE, SR.

Founder and Administrator of
Business Champions Linked for Christ
Co-Founder of Supernatural Evangelism Int.
Co-Founder & Sr. Pastor of Doors of Destiny Savannah, GA

TRILOGY
A WHOLLY OWNED SUBSIDIARY OF TBN
PROFESSIONAL PUBLISHING MEETS POWERFUL PROMOTION

I'm a New Creation... Now What?

Trilogy Christian Publishers
A Wholly Owned Subsidiary of Trinity Broadcasting Network
2442 Michelle Drive, Tustin, CA 92780

Copyright © 2024 by Lyndle Savage, Sr.

Scripture quotations marked (NLT) are taken from the Holy Bible, New Living Translation, copyright © 1996, 2004, 2015 by Tyndale House Foundation. Used by permission of Tyndale House Publishers, Inc., Carol Stream, Illinois 60188. All rights reserved.

Scripture quotations marked (GNT) are taken from the Good News Translation® (Today's English Version, Second Edition). Copyright © 1982 American Bible Society. All rights reserved.

Scripture quotations marked (CEV) are taken from the Contemporary English Version®. Copyright © 1995 American Bible Society. All rights reserved.

Scripture quotations marked (ESV) are taken from the ESV® Bible (The Holy Bible, English Standard Version®), copyright © 2001 by Crossway Bibles, a publishing ministry of Good News Publishers. Used by permission. All rights reserved.

Scripture quotations marked (NCV) are taken from the New Century Version®. Copyright © 2005 by Thomas Nelson. Used by permission. All rights reserved.

Scripture quotations marked (GW) are taken from GOD'S WORD®, © 1995 God's Word to the Nations. Used by permission of God's Word Mission Society.

Scripture quotations marked (NKJV) are taken from the New King James Version®. Copyright © 1982 by Thomas Nelson. Used by permission. All rights reserved.

Scripture marked (VOICE) are taken from The Voice™. Copyright © 2012 by Ecclesia Bible Society. Used by permission. All rights reserved.

Scripture quotations marked (HCSB) are taken from the Holman Christian Standard Bible®, Copyright © 1999, 2000, 2002, 2003, 2009 by Holman Bible Publishers. Used by permission. Holman Christian Standard Bible®, Holman CSB®, and HCSB® are federally registered trademarks of Holman Bible Publishers.

Scripture quotations marked (TLB) are taken from The Living Bible copyright © 1971. Used by permission of Tyndale House Publishers, a Division of Tyndale House Ministries, Carol Stream, Illinois 60188. All rights reserved.

Scripture quotations marked (KJV) are taken from the King James Version of the Bible. Public domain.

For information, address Trilogy Christian Publishing Rights Department, 2442 Michelle Drive, Tustin, CA 92780. Trilogy Christian Publishing/ TBN and colophon are trademarks of Trinity Broadcasting Network. For information about special discounts for bulk purchases, please contact Trilogy Christian Publishing.

Trilogy Disclaimer: The views and content expressed in this book are those of the author and may not necessarily reflect the views and doctrine of Trilogy Christian Publishing or the Trinity Broadcasting Network.

10 9 8 7 6 5 4 3 2 1
Library of Congress Cataloging-in-Publication Data is available.

ISBN: 979-8-89041-965-1
ISBN: 979-8-89041-966-8 (eBook)

"Helping you fulfill
Christ's great commission;
to set captives free, heal the sick,
and redeem the lost."

Special Thanks

I want to express my warmest appreciation to five individuals whose input and support made this project possible.

Firstly, to my wife, Jackie, whose sacrifices are too numerous to mention so that I could devote time and energy to the writing of this book.

Secondly, to my secondary English teacher, spiritual cheerleader, childhood babysitter, mentor, friend, and Aunt Rita (Savage) Wallace. She provided the first proof reading and grammatical edits. I cannot thank you enough for all you have done throughout my whole life to show support and guidance!

Thirdly, Dr. Joe Cathy who provided proof reading/additional editing and scholarly insights that were invaluable.

And lastly, to Diane and Farley Dunn, I want to thank them for their encouragement (Diane) and (Farley) additional proof reading and masterful editing to get this manuscript ready for publication submittal.

Dedication

I want to dedicate this, my first book, to the loving memory of my parents (Dad) Maxie L. Savage and (Mother) Joveda A. Savage. They were my bedrock, on whose faith, dedication, and devotion to our Lord and Savior were lifelong examples to me and countless others. They encouraged and supported me during the writing of this book, but unfortunately did not survive to see its publication.

Table of Contents

Special Thanks v
Dedication vii

Introduction 11
Commit Yourself to a Bible-Believing,
      Faith-Building Local Church 13
Build Solid Friendships with Strong Christians 19
Read and Study Your Bible Daily 23
Pray Regularly 33
Worship Routinely 47
Tithe 71
Share Christ with Others 85
Final Thoughts 95

Copyrights 99

Introduction

So, you have committed to follow Christ and to give Him your life. Second Corinthians 5:17 tells us,

> ¹⁷ *Whoever is a believer in Christ is a new creation. The old way of living has disappeared. A new way of living has come into existence.* (GW)

As a new creation, you are now like a baby—spiritually speaking. Jesus Himself tells us in John 3:3b,

> ³ *"…Unless someone is born again, he cannot see the kingdom of God"* (HCSB)

And He also says Matthew 18:3b…

> ³ *"…unless you are converted and become as little children, you will by no means enter the kingdom of heaven"* (NKJV)

As you begin your new spiritual life in Christ, you will need to "grow up" or mature in spiritual development. A way to look at this is when you were born you began to grow up physically and mature emotionally; this process occurs somewhat naturally. However, in order to develop physically and emotionally, you needed certain things for the process to occur in a healthy and successful manner. You needed a safe environment, social interaction with peers, appropriate nutrition, emotional support, modeled behavior, physical activity, and unconditional love.

In most cases, these seven growth and developmental necessities are provided by and through the supervision of our parents. In this book, you will learn the seven necessities for your spiritual development. You will see the characteristics for spiritual growth and development are very similar to those for physical growth and emotional development. You will discover things which will greatly enhance your physical and/or emotional health by comparing the seven attributes required for spiritual maturity with the seven necessities of physical growth and emotional development.

The seven attributes required for healthy spiritual maturity are:

1. Commit to a Bible believing, faith building, local church.
2. Build solid friendships with strong Christians.
3. Read and Study the Bible daily.
4. Pray regularly.
5. Worship routinely.
6. Tithe
7. Share what Christ has done for you with others.

Commit Yourself to a Bible-Believing, Faith-Building Local Church

SAFE ENVIRONMENT

Committing yourself to a Bible believing, faith building, local church compares directly to providing a newborn with a safe environment. When a new baby arrives, many parents will go through their home and move or discard unsafe things. These same new parents will install electrical plug covers, child safety locks on cabinets, and other such safety mechanisms which are needed as the child grows. Why? The answer is obvious—it is to provide a home which is a safe environment for the child to grow and play.

There are four key elements to creating a spiritually safe environment:

1. The members must demonstrate strong commitments to one another.
2. The Bible must be the absolute authority for teaching and doctrine.

3. Services and events will improve our knowledge of God and strengthen our faith.
4. The church must be local.

Let's explore the need for a local church first. Is it really important for it to be local? Yes, and here are a few of reasons why: For one, and probably most importantly, it is the lifestyle Jesus modeled for us. In Luke 4:16, we see Jesus attended services regularly.

> [16] *Then Jesus came to Nazareth, where he had been brought up. As usual he went into the synagogue on the day of rest—a holy day. He stood up to read the lesson.* (GW)

In this passage the phrase, "As usual he went into the synagogue on the day of rest – a holy day" plainly indicates Jesus attended services weekly. Jesus is the example for all Christians to follow, thus it is our privilege to attend services weekly. From a commonsense perspective, for any church to serve your growing spiritual needs, you need to physically attend services and functions without a great deal of time and/or travel. We see this model in scripture in Acts 5:42,

> [42] *And daily in the temple, and in every house, they did not cease teaching and preaching Jesus as the Christ.* (NKJV)

As well as in Hebrews 3:12 – 13,

> [12] *Be careful, brothers and sisters, that none of you ever develop a wicked, unbelieving heart that turns away from the living God.* [13] *Encourage each other every day while you have the opportunity. If you do this, none of you will be deceived by sin and become stubborn.* (GW)

In these scriptures, we see the example of early Christians who spent time together on a regular basis. All believers need a spiritual family which is close enough to see daily, if necessary. A geographically "local" church is important because it can help us to form relationships providing vital spiritual support for the well-being of all its members.

Our second key element of an effective local church is it must improve our knowledge of God and strengthen our faith. We are instructed to hold fast to our faith by attending church.

> [23] *We must continue to hold firmly to our declaration of faith. The one who made the promise is faithful.*
> [24] *We must also consider how to encourage each other to show love and to do good things.* [25] *We should not stop gathering together with other believers, as some of you are doing. Instead, we must continue to encourage each other even more as we see the day of the Lord coming.*
> — Hebrews 10:23 – 25a (GW)

As 1 Thessalonians 5:11 says, *"comfort yourselves together, and edify one another…"* (KJV), instructing us to edify or build up one another. Edify—from the Greek word "οἰκοδομέω" (oikodomeo) and pronounced {oy-kod-om-eh'-o}—means "to promote growth in Christian wisdom, affection, grace, virtue, holiness, and blessedness."

One of the main purposes of attending a local church is to assist in building or strengthening our faith. From these passages, it is evident through our spiritual family, we are inspired to love deeper and to perform greater acts of kindness. Thus, we must contribute to building each other's faith; which, in turn creates a safe environment for positive spiritual growth and development.

Just a note of caution—there are groups out there calling themselves churches; but, in fact, they are not faith building. Before you commit to a body, make sure they biblically inspire and challenge you to strive to better exemplify the life and love of Christ. If there is not a church near you which meets these conditions you should consider inviting anyone you know who has made the same commitment to Christ to get together regularly to read and study the Bible, worship, and build relationships.

A church who proclaims the absolute authority of the Bible for teaching and doctrine is the third consideration for determining the appropriateness of a spiritual family. Just as emotional development can be distorted in a dysfunctional family, the same is true of the spiritual family. True spiritual growth can only occur in a body dedicated to God in the appropriate manner. The appropriate manner is demonstrated by the Christians of the Bible in Acts 2:42,

> ⁴² *And they continued steadfastly in the apostles' doctrine and fellowship, and in breaking of bread, and in prayers.* (KJV)

The "apostles' doctrines" is recorded in what we now call the New Testament.

Second Timothy 3:16 demonstrates the validity of the Bible for everyday living:

> *All scripture is given by inspiration of God, and is profitable for doctrine, for reproof, for correction, for instruction in righteousness.* (NKJV)

Throughout scripture we see the church referred to as the House of God or the House of the Lord, so it is the church which mirrors the home. As it is with a family home, so it is with a church. Obviously, the structure is not what is important. When a family acquires a new home, do they leave the baby at the previous house? Absolutely not! A church is not a building; it is a family! For any group to be a healthy family, they must be committed to one another. It is this commitment to one another which creates the safe environment!!

My older brother firmly believed it was his right to pick on me; however, no one outside the family was afforded such privileges. In fact, he would (and did) fight neighborhood bullies, who were bigger and older than he, for picking on me! Most of the time, he won; but in all cases the bullies left me alone thereafter.

One of my younger brother's buddies once told me a story about him and his older brother. The younger had spoken offensively to some of the kids at their neighborhood hangout. Afterward, he came to get his older brother's help in the fight which was brewing. The older brother's words to his younger brother made a point about family in a manner I will never forget. "I got your back, and whether we win this fight or not, when it's over and we get home, I'm gonna beat you up one side and down the other for get'n me into this!!!"

That's family! It's this family attitude which creates the safe environment! They will always "have your back" against your enemies, but they will also let you know when you step out of line. Committing yourself to a local family of faith-building, Bible-believers who give back this type of commitment to you; is the first step in your spiritual growth and development.

Build Solid Friendships with Strong Christians

SOCIAL INTERACTION WITH PEERS

Just as social interaction with peers is critical to natural development so is building solid friendships with strong Christians to our spiritual development. While it is true experts in child development will disagree on many minor points, and yet none would disagree with all humans by nature are social beings. Most would agree we learn certain things exclusively from our peers, and the influence of peers is far greater than any other mechanism of learning. There is an extensive list of research articles supporting the notion of children learning better in groups of their peers rather than by traditional instruction from a teacher. In any case, we instinctively understand it is important for children to socialize with other children in order to develop healthily. The same is true of our spiritual development.

We know we are created by God in His likeness and image by reading Genesis 1:26 – 27.

> ²⁶ *Then God said, "Let us make human beings in our image, to be like us. They will reign over the fish in the sea, the birds in the sky, the livestock, all the wild animals on the earth, and the small animals that scurry along the ground."*
>
> ²⁷ *So God created human beings in his own image. In the image of God he created them; male and female he created them.* (NLT)

We also know God "is love" by looking at 1 John 4:8.

> ⁸ *But if a person isn't loving and kind, it shows that he doesn't know God – for God is love.* (TLB)

Since God "is" love, then He "is" social in His nature; and, therefore, He created you and me to be social as well. In fact, the Bible teaches us to bond with other believers to the point our group can be compared to a human body. This bond created by each member supplying their uniqueness to the group and makes the whole better than the sum of its parts.

> *Just as there are many parts to our bodies, so it is with Christ's body. We are all parts of it, and it takes every one of us to make it complete, for we each have different work to do. So we belong to each other, and each needs all the others.*
>
> — Romans 12:4 – 5 (TLB)

And Ephesians 4:15 – 16 informs us to socialize in a tight group of strong believers, we are growing up to be like Christ.

15 Love should always make us tell the truth. Then we will grow in every way and be more like Christ, the head 16 of the body. Christ holds it together and makes all of its parts work perfectly, as it grows and becomes strong because of love. (CEV)

I'm sure you have heard the old saying, "Birds of a feather flock together," which simply means we become like those with whom we spend our time. There is biblical truth in this old statement, as evidenced in Proverbs 13:20:

20 He who walks with wise men will be wise, But the companion of fools will be destroyed. (NKJV)

This is why it is vitally important to spend face time with strong believers. Make the choice to find quality committed Christian friends and then spend time together. God makes his attitude about friendships very clear in James 4:4.

4 So, you are not loyal to God! You should know that loving the world is the same as hating God. Anyone who wants to be a friend of the world becomes God's enemy. (NCV)

We should not turn away from sinners, but we should not spend an abundance of time with those whose lifestyles would tempt us to falter in our pursuit of holiness. Actually, as we will see a little later, we are commanded by Christ to interact with the world around us to be a positive influence rather than being influenced by the world and its sinful ways.

A wise man will listen and increase his learning, and a discerning man will obtain guidance.

— Proverbs 1:5 (HCSB)

A wise man is mightier than a strong man. Wisdom is mightier than strength. Don't go to war without wise guidance; there is safety in many counselors.

— Proverbs 24:5 – 6 (TLB)

For our own safety, we find God's word tells us to seek those who are more skillful in the things of God. As we undertake this new creation life in Christ, we will have opposition. Therefore, we find strength, instruction, and assistance from godly relationships. God made us social beings, and we are stronger in groups than we would ever be as individuals. Don't hesitate to reach out to those around you who are strong in their faith.

YOU WILL BE GLAD YOU DID!!!!

Read and Study Your Bible Daily

APPROPRIATE NUTRITION

Everyone should agree proper nutrition is essential for our physical and emotional development. Just as infants must begin with milk or formula and progress ultimately to full table foods in order to develop physically, so must we consume our spiritual nutrition to grow our inner man. The Bible compares the Word of God to milk for babies in 1 Peter 2:1 – 3.

> [1] *So get rid of every kind of evil, every kind of deception, hypocrisy, jealousy, and every kind of slander.* [2] *Desire God's pure word as newborn babies desire milk. Then you will grow in your salvation.* [3] *Certainly you have tasted that the Lord is good!* (GW)

We are also told God's word is something worthwhile to eat in Jeremiah 15:16.

> [16] *Your words are what sustain me; they are food to my hungry soul. They bring joy to my sorrowing heart and delight me. How proud I am to bear your name, O Lord.* (TLB)

God's word is said to be strong meat capable of teaching us to perceive the difference between good and evil.

> ¹² *You have been Christians for a long time now, and you ought to be teaching others, but instead you have dropped back to the place where you need someone to teach you all over again the very first principles of God's word. You are like babies who can drink only milk, not old enough for solid food.* ¹³ *And when a person is still living on milk it shows he isn't very far along in the Christian life, and doesn't know much about the difference between right and wrong. He is still a baby-Christian!* ¹⁴ *You will never be able to eat solid spiritual food and understand the deeper things of God's word until you become better Christians and learn right from wrong by practicing doing right.*
>
> — Hebrews 5:12 – 14 (TLB)

From these passages of scripture, we gain the understanding of God's word as the substance of our spiritual nutrition throughout our entire life. Because the word of God is dynamic and supernatural, it is milk, strained fruits and vegetables, and meat—all at the same time. This means as you mature spiritually, God's word will open to you in new ways to meet your changing spiritual needs. In other words, we need to feed on it like we would physical food… daily. There are many reasons why reading and studying the Bible is as critically important as appropriate nutrition for a growing child. Let's look at just a few.

> *For the word of God is full of living power. It is sharper than the sharpest knife, cutting deep into our innermost thoughts and desires. It exposes us for what we really are.*
>
> — Hebrews 4:12 (NLT 1996)

This verse supports the notion mentioned earlier of God's word as dynamic and supernatural. However, it goes even further to inform us it is alive and is capable of empowering us to differentiate between our thoughts and God's. As we become increasingly familiar with God's word, which reveals His thoughts, it only makes sense His voice becomes easier to hear and understand. Also, as we read the Bible, we are exposed to God's personality, and His gentle and quiet promptings are more easily recognizable.

> *I have hidden Your Word in my heart, that I might not sin against You.*
>
> — Psalms 119:11 (NLT)

This passage is self explanatory: the more of God's word we have in our heart, the less likely we are to fall victim to sin's temptation. Therefore, we need to realize as we expose our minds to the illumination of the Bible, it enlightens us to the changes needed in our lives. However, unlike traditional education, it also empowers us to make the changes it reveals. When we look into the mirror of scripture, we see not only ourselves with our weaknesses and shortcomings, but also as a new creature created in Christ we will also see God is inside of us, and by His strength He enables us to do all things.

> *I can do all things through Christ who strengthens me.*
>
> — Philippians 4:13 (NKJV)

In light of this truth God's word suddenly makes much more sense. Surrendering your life to the Lordship of Jesus Christ is just the beginning of a marvelous and awesome adventure into fulfilling all the unimaginable things God uniquely hand-crafted you to perform.

God's word dynamically illuminates; revealing the real states of our hearts and minds!

> *Your word is a lamp to my feet*
> *And a light to my path.*
>
> — Psalms 119:105 (NKJV)

In this passage, the Bible is shown to be both like a lamp and a high intensity flashlight. This is divinely important as both an instrument to reveal our current position as well as shining a beam of light through the darkness in the direction of travel. This means scripture, when appropriately used, will open to our understanding who and what we are at this moment in time. Then it clearly points to the best path for life.

A lamp spreads light over a selected area thus making normal activities possible. However, a flashlight focuses light in a beam, which helps to see long distances. When we gain proficiency in utilizing the Word of God, it will act as both a lamp to successfully handle the immediate needs of our spiritual life as well as acting as a flashlight to reveal God's direction for our life.

> *Do your best to present yourself to God as one approved, a worker who has no need to be ashamed, rightly handling the word of truth.*
>
> — 2 Timothy 2:15 (ESV)

Here, we gain the understanding, the more of God's word we know creates in us the ability to stand before God without feeling inadequate. Often times, as we first get to know anyone new, we are a bit cautious about what to say and not to say. The same is true in a relationship with our Heavenly Father; however, through the knowledge of His Word, we become increasingly familiar with Him, and we get to know what He likes and dislikes. As we get to know Him intimately, we can do as Hebrews 4:16b says:

> [16] *…come boldly to the throne of grace, that we may obtain mercy and find grace to help in time of need.* (NKJV)

> [14] *No, it is here with you. You know it and can quote it, so now obey it.* [15] *"Today I am giving you a choice between good and evil, between life and death.* [16] *If you obey the commands of the* LORD *your God, which I give you today, if you love him, obey him, and keep all his laws, then you will prosper and become a nation of*

many people. The L*ord* *your God will bless you in the land that you are about to occupy.*

19 I am now giving you the choice between life and death, between God's blessing and God's curse, and I call heaven and earth to witness the choice you make. Choose life. 20 Love the L*ord* *your God, obey him and be faithful to him, and then you and your descendants will live long in the land."*

— Deuteronomy 30:14 – 16, 19 – 20a (GNT)

The important thing to notice in this passage of scripture is we are not spectators in life but active partners with God Almighty in the outcome of our lives. As we gain knowledge of His Holy Word, it changes our perception; and thus, it also changes how we speak about the world around us. As we learn to view ourselves and others the way God sees us, we become increasingly capable of changing our world by the power of God working in and through us.

This power comes from knowing Him intimately and obeying His direction. In fact, Jesus tells us in Mark 11:22 – 24 if we have faith we will speak to our problems, and they must obey.

22 Then Jesus said to His disciples, "Have faith in God. 23 I assure you that you can say too this mountain, 'May God lift you up and throw you into the sea,' and your command will be obeyed. All that's required is that you really believe and do not doubt in your heart. 24 Listen to me! You can pray for anything, and if you believe, you will have it. (NLT)

Romans 10:17 (ESV) informs us faith comes from knowing God's word: "So faith comes from hearing, and hearing through the word of Christ."

> *² But they delight in the law of the Lord,*
> *meditating on it day and night.*
> *³ They are like trees planted along the riverbank,*
> *bearing fruit each season.*
> *Their leaves never wither,*
> *and they prosper in all they do.*
>
> — Psalms 1:2 – 3 (NLT)

As we get to the place where we enjoy the Word of God and spend every possible moment in God's Word, it transforms our lives, so we become stable and productive. In this passage, those who read and study the word are compared to well-watered trees; these conditions produce trees with thriving root systems, which are then capable of absorbing nutrition, even in drought conditions. Life happens, and hard times come to everyone, but those who have learned and are skillful in God's Word will continue to thrive and survive. Water your spirit-man and you will thrive according to God's plans and purposes!

Below, I have included a daily Bible reading plan which will take about thirty to forty minutes per day to read the New Testament in thirty days. Every day before you read, you should ask the Lord to guide your thoughts and teach you what He wants you to learn. It is also advisable to have a seasoned believer you can call with questions about your reading. If you have followed the teaching in this book, you will have made friends with strong followers of Christ which you can ask for assistance with your spiritual education. Upon completing the New Testament in thirty days it would greatly benefit you as a new Christian to select other translations to read and repeating the reading plan again every thirty days. If you will spend about twenty minutes a day reading in the Old Testament you be able to read the entire Old Testament in six months. So, in one hour per day reading your Bible you will read the entire Bible twice in one year and the New Testament twelve times, your spiritual growth will be astounding!

30 DAY NEW CREATION BIBLE READING PLAN

1. Matthew 1:1 – 9:38
2. Matthew 10:1 – 16:28
3. Matthew 17:1 – 24:27
4. Matthew 24:28 – Mark 1:27
5. Mark 1:28 – 8:27
6. Mark 8:28 – 14:48
7. Mark 14:49 – Luke 4:11
8. Luke 4:12 – 9:37
9. Luke 9:38 – 15:29
10. Luke 15:30 – 22:50
11. Luke 22:51 – John 4:54
12. John 5:1 – 10:42
13. John 11:1 – 18:33
14. John 18:34 – Acts 4:37
15. Acts 5:1 – 11:16
16. Acts 11:17 – 18:18

17. Acts 18:19 – 25:27
18. Acts 26:1 – Romans 6:16
19. Romans 6:17 – 15:33
20. Romans 16:1 – 1 Corinthians 10:33
21. 1 Corinthians 11:1 – 2 Corinthians 5:21
22. 2 Corinthians 6:1 – Galatians 4:31
23. Galatians 5:1 – Philippians 3:21
24. Philippians 4:1 – 2 Thessalonians 3:18
25. 1 Timothy 1:1 – Philemon 1:25
26. Hebrews 1:1 – 11:23
27. Hebrews 11:24 – 1 Peter 3:22
28. 1 Peter 4:1 – Jude 1:25
29. Revelation 1:1 – 12:17
30. Revelation 13:1 – 22:21

Now let's look at studying the Word of God because there is a significant difference between reading and studying. Reading provides context and understanding on a broad level, while studying opens the subtle detail levels of understanding. Just as there is a difference between how we read a novel versus how we read a textbook, so it is with reading and studying the Bible. Because God's Word is a supernatural book, we need to approach it both ways—it needs to be read for context as well as studied for depth of understanding. Let's examine probably the most common methodology for Bible study, called a word study.

A word study, as the name implies, collects all the scripture references which utilize a particular word or phrase. Then, when read together, it provides a deeper understanding about the defined topic. First, let me state very clearly you DO NOT need training in Latin, Greek nor Hebrew, but you will need some extra tools, in addition to your Bible. You will need a good concordance like *Strong's Exhaustive Concordance*. However, if you have access to a computer connected to the internet or a smart phone, you can download great Bible study programs and/or apps. Check out www.blueletterBible.org, and www.Biblegateway.com for your computer; MySword for Android tablets and smart phones; and Logos Bible or Bible.is apps for iPhone, iPad, and iPod touches. These programs take a little practice, but they provide even the most novice student with a wealth of easily understandable information.

Pray Regularly

EMOTIONAL SUPPORT

Prayer is the spiritual equivalence of emotional support because it is in prayer where we pour out our heart to God. It is where we talk openly and take our true thoughts to the Lord, and He patiently listens. We express our needs, shortcomings, and our innermost feelings. As we gain experience in prayer, we begin to pray the words we find in the scriptures. (We discovered earlier the word of God reveals the will of God.)

As we become increasingly skillful in understanding and knowledge of the Word of God, we will greatly enhance our effectiveness in prayer. The better we know our spouses, the easier it becomes to communicate with him/her. Just as marital communication must be two-directional, meaning it is a conversation where both people speak and listen, so is prayer. We both speak to God and listen to His reply. He does and will speak.

Merriam-Webster.com defines the word pray in following ways:

Transitive verb
- 1: ENTREAT, IMPLORE —often used as a function word in introducing a question, request, or plea <*pray* be careful>

- 2: to get or bring by praying

Intransitive verb
- 1: to make a request in a humble manner
- 2: to address God or a god with adoration, confession, supplication, or thanksgiving

Now let's look at how Jesus taught us (His disciples) to pray. Jesus tells us repeatedly to pray to the Father in His name. Let's look at some quotes from Jesus which supports this statement.

> [12] *I am telling you the truth: those who believe in me will do what I do—yes, they will do even greater things, because I am going to the Father.* [13] *And I will do whatever you ask for in my name, so that the Father's glory will be shown through the Son.* [14] *If you ask me for anything in my name, I will do it.* [15] *"If you love me, you will obey my commandments."*
>
> —John 14:12 – 15

Here we understand through prayer, we are empowered to do the works Jesus did, and also to reach for more than He did! That's a bold statement because He did many mighty, amazing, and miraculous things. The encouragement here is guard your faith, don't allow the experiences of others to determine your outcomes. Reach into God's abundance and believe Him for greater things bringing glory, honor, and adoration to Him.

It would be irresponsible not to discuss a critical connection from this passage between answered prayers and obedience to His commands. However, let me state very clearly obedience **IS NOT** a difficult concept. **IT IS NOT** strict adherence to a massive list of "thou shalt nots", nor does obedience require endless recitations. It does require dedicated listening to the voice of your conscience, which is actually the Holy Spirit speaking to you, and then follow those leadings. It is truly simple—Jesus's commandments are few and easily understandable.

> [34] *So I give you a new command: Love each other deeply and fully. Remember the ways that I have loved you, and demonstrate your love for others in those same ways.* [35] *Everyone will know you as My followers if you demonstrate your love to others.*
>
> — John 13:34 – 35 (VOICE)

Here in John chapter 13, Jesus gave one (1) commandment to His disciples, which is to love others. This is actually the same conversation and teaching of Jesus we were already looking at in John Chapter 14.

Let's backtrack for a moment and set the stage for this entire discussion. John chapters 13 through 17 shows Jesus spending time with His closest disciples on His last night before He died to save them (as well as us) from sin. He is pouring out all He is to them by summing up the most important things He has taught from their whole time together. Think of it this way—what would you say to your closest friends if you knew tomorrow was your last day in this life?

This is exactly what Jesus is doing here. He is instructing His closest people on what are the most important things for them to remember and think about from His life and ministry. Jesus spends a great deal of His last night discussing and illustrating how to pray; therefore, He must have thought it crucial! Carefully crafted into every teaching on prayer was this underlying theme of love; love and prayer are like the threads of the finest fabrics delicately woven together.

The disciples had heard Jesus teach on the commandment of love before, several times in fact. One of those times, Jesus told them "ALL" the commandments from the teachings of Moses, as well as all the Old Testament prophets, were based on and fulfilled by the commandment of love. We see this in Matthew chapter 22.

> *36 "Teacher, which is the most important commandment in the law of Moses?"*
>
> *37 Jesus replied, "'You must love the Lord your God with all you heart, all your soul, and all your mind.' 38 This is the first and greatest commandment. 39 A second is equally important: 'Love your neighbor as yourself.' 40 All the other commandments and all the demands of the prophets are based on these two commandments."*
>
> — Matthew 22:36 – 40 (NLT)

In this example of Jesus's teaching, we see we are also to love God with everything we are, as well as loving others. When we truly love, we cannot take the object of our love for granted, nor would we harm them in any way. If we love God, we won't sin against Him; if we love others, we won't sin against them.

Paul the Apostle was a classically trained practitioner and teacher of the Judaic Laws. As a follower of Christ and one of the greatest teachers of the New Testament, he taught all the commandments of God listed in the Old Testament are accomplished by loving others in his letter to church of Galatia.

> *[13] For, dear brothers, you have been given freedom: not freedom to do wrong, but freedom to love and serve each other. [14] For the whole Law can be summed up in this one command: "Love others as you love yourself."*
>
> — Galatians 5:13 – 14 (TLB)

In John chapter 15, Jesus continues His instructions on prayer and obedience to the love command. He also informs His disciples not to think of themselves as servants, but friends. This is important as we approach God in prayer; we are to do so, as comfortably as talking to our best friend.

Some people approach prayer as though they are slaves begging some malevolent master for special favors. However, Jesus teaches us to come to God as confident friends.

> *[14] And you are my friends, if you obey me. [15] Servants don't know what their master is doing, and so I don't speak to you as my servants. I speak to you as my friends, and I have told you everything that my Father has told me. [16] You did not choose me. I chose you and sent you out to produce fruit, the kind of fruit that will last. Then my Father will give you whatever*

you ask for in my name. [17] *So I command you to love each other.*

— John 15:14 – 17 (CEV)

This passage shows effective prayers are also contingent on our productivity. This simply means we are living our life according to His plan. (We will explore producing lasting fruit in greater detail in the final section of this book.)

Jesus has more to say about prayer in John Chapter 16, where He compares our struggles in this life to birth pains. He compares answered prayer to the satisfaction a new mother feels when her baby is born. In making this comparison, He is preparing His disciples for the time of His death and ascension into heaven because after His death and ascension, the disciples will have to pray for themselves.

Consider it like a parent preparing a child to ride a bicycle without the training wheels. In this portion of scripture, Jesus gives us some very specific instructions on how to pray.

> [21] *When a woman is about to give birth, she is sad because her hour of suffering has come; but when the baby is born, she forgets her suffering, because she is happy that a baby has been born into the world.* [22] *That is how it is with you: now you are sad, but I will see you again, and your hearts will be filled with gladness, the kind of gladness that no one can take away from you.* [23] *When that day comes, you will not ask me for anything. I am telling you the truth: the Father will give you whatever you ask of him in my name.* [24] *Until now you have not asked for anything*

> *in my name; ask and you will receive, so that your happiness may be complete.* ²⁵ *I have used figures of to speech to tell you these things. But the time will come when I will not use figures of speech, but will speak to you plainly about the Father.* ²⁶ *When that day comes, you will ask him in my name; and I do not say that I will ask him on your behalf,* ²⁷ *for the Father himself loves you. He loves you because you love me and have believed that I came from God.*
>
> — John 16:21 – 27 (GNT)

Jesus makes it very clear we are to pray directly to the Father, and we are not even to pray to Jesus. However, we are to pray in His name. From this reading, it is abundantly evident the practice of praying to a departed saint is not scriptural.

Then Jesus goes on to tell us why we are to pray directly to the Father— is because God the Father loves each of us individually, as much as He loves Jesus. Praying to Jesus would be like asking a sibling to speak to our earthly dad for us. In some instances, people have asked siblings talk to their parents on their behalf because they were afraid, perhaps due to an action they knew would be displeasing to the parent. (Unfortunately, some have emotionally unhealthy parents which placed unjustified fear in their children.) However, God is a perfect and loving parent, and there is never a need to fear Him. He wants us to always come directly to him with our needs, concerns, or mistakes.

Just hours before His crucifixion, Jesus spends His final moments with His closest disciples, instructing them on how to live, love, and pray. He gave them a tremendous amount of guidance on how to pray as has been illustrated in chapters 14, 15, and 16 of John's gospel. In chapter 17, the entire chapter is John quoting the prayer Jesus prayed.

He taught them about prayer, and now He gives a living example of prayer. Chapter 17 models some key aspects for the structure and sequence of effective prayer. (Chapter 17 will not be reprinted here, but the reader is highly encouraged to read this chapter in its entirety.)

In the first part of verse 1, when He addresses Him as Father, Jesus first acknowledges who God is. The Bible tells us Jesus was the first of many brothers.

> *For from the very beginning God decided that those who came to him—and all along he knew who would—should become like his Son, so that his Son would be the First, with many brothers.*
>
> — Romans 8:29 (TLB)

> *The Spirit himself testifies with our spirit that we are God's children.*
>
> — Romans 8:16 (GW)

Next, from the remaining portion of John 17:1 through the end of verse 3, Jesus acknowledges what God has done. We do this by acknowledging what God has done in our lives as well as acknowledge Him as Creator and Ruler of the Universe. We can pray the Psalms, which glorifies God for who He is, and what He has done.

Thirdly, Jesus talks about what He has done in John 17:4 – 8. This is where we would tell Him about our struggles and confess our sins. We pour out our hearts about our lives and what we are facing, not in a griping nor complaining sort of way; we just simply and honestly tell Him about our situations. Even though He already knows everything, we just need to open our hearts and verbally express our deepest thoughts and feelings to Him. These actions of vulnerability, prepares our hearts to receive from God Almighty.

The fourth segment in the sequence of effective prayer illustrated by Jesus is to pray for those close to us. He prayed in John 17:9 – 18 for His disciples; these are the ones He considered as His family. He asked God to grant them peace in troubled times; strength to face any and all difficulties; protection from the evil one, and love to bind these friends in faith. We are to follow Christ's example and pray for our family and friends.

The fifth element exemplified by our Lord in prayer is found in John 17:19 – 24. This is where He makes His requests to God the Father. Notice Jesus spends far more time praying for others rather than praying for Himself: This is key to effective prayer. We are told in James 4:3

> [3] *Yet even when you do pray, your prayers are not answered, because you pray just for selfish reasons.*
> (CEV)

Self-centered prayers are not answered. Jesus teaches in Matthew 6:33 we should pray in a way which "seeks first" God's Kingdom, which then allows God's blessings to fulfill our personal desires. This is in stark contrast to the way most of us are inclined to pray. However, Philippians 4:6 tells us to make our request to God with thanksgiving. This means we are to ask for things important to us; and yet, they should be kept in proper perspective.

Attribute number six portrayed by Jesus Christ in John 17:25. This is where He acknowledges God the Father's nature and character. When we follow this pattern and pray in faith, in accordance with the Father's will, we can expect God's help.

> *So we can go confidently to the throne of God's kindness to receive mercy and find kindness, which will help us at the right time.*
>
> — Hebrews 4:16 (GW)

> [13] *I am writing this to you so that you may know that you have eternal life—you that believe in the Son of God.* [14] *We have courage in God's presence, because we are sure that he hears us if we ask him for anything that is according to his will.* [15] *He hears us whenever we ask him; and since we know this is true, we know also that he gives us what we ask from him.*
>
> — 1 John 5: 13 – 15 (GW)

How do we know we are praying according to the Father's will?

> *In the beginning was the Word, and the Word was with God, and the Word was God.*
>
> — John 1:1 (NKJV)

> *Make them holy for Yourself by the truth. Your Word is truth.*
>
> — John 17:17 (NLV)

> *13 When God made his promise to Abraham, he made a vow to do what he had promised. Since there was no one greater than himself, he used his own name when he made his vow. … 16 When we make a vow, we use the name of someone greater than ourselves, and the vow settles all arguments. 17 To those who were to receive what he promised, God wanted to make it very clear that he would never change his purpose; so he added his vow to the promise.*
>
> — Hebrews 6:13, 16 – 17 (GNT)

These passages from God's word reveal God, His will, and His word are all one and the same. Therefore, as we pray the scriptures in our prayers, we can be confident we are praying according to His will.

Our loving Savior demonstrated the seventh and final aspect of appropriate prayer in John 17:26. This is where He declares His commitment to fulfill His God-given purpose. As we pray, we too must declare our wholehearted commitment to obey God's Word, His will, and His voice.

Prayer quickly becomes a conversation where we speak, and God speaks back. Don't be alarmed or confused by the notion of God speaking to you, it's really not complicated. Let's look at some scripture which supports the claim of God speaking to us.

> *Know that the LORD, He is God;*
> *It is He who has made us, and not we ourselves;*
> *We are His people and the sheep of His pasture.*
>
> — Psalms 100:3 (NKJV)

> *[3] The guard who is posted to protect the sheep opens the gate for the shepherd, and the sheep hear his voice. He calls his own sheep by name and leads them out. [4] When all the sheep have been gathered, he walks on ahead of them; and they follow him because they know his voice. [5] The sheep would not be willing to follow a stranger; they run because they do not know the voice of a stranger.*
>
> — John 10: 3 – 5 (VOICE)

> *[7] He is our God;*
> *we are the people he cares for,*
> *the flock for which he provides.*
> *Listen today to what he says…*
>
> — Psalms 95:7 (GNT)

The way this works on a practical level is by comparing it to the time in your childhood when you disobeyed. You might have had the thought, *I shouldn't do this because I will get in trouble.* God's voice was speaking to you and convicting you of His directions for your life at that moment. We all can hear His voice and the more we obey His voice the easier it becomes to hear!

This is not the only way which God speaks to us; but, for most, it is the primary method God uses. Just remember God, His word, and His will are the same which means His voice will not speak anything contrary to His word.

Worship Routinely

MODELED BEHAVIOR

Worship may not be what most commonly think of as worship. Most probably think of a meeting filled with people singing and then someone shares a teaching from scripture; well this could be an expression of worship, but this is not the full description of worship. Once we understand what it means to truly worship God, we will then understand how it is comparable with modeled behavior.

WORSHIP (FROM THE GREEK)

proskuneó: to do reverence to

- Original Word: προσκυνέω
- Part of Speech: Verb
- Transliteration: proskuneó
- Phonetic Spelling: (pros-koo-neh'-o)
- Definition: to do reverence to
- Usage: I go down on my knees to, do obeisance to, worship.

HELPS Word-studies

- 4352 *proskynéō* (from 4314 /*prós*, "towards" and *kyneo*, "*to kiss*") – properly, to kiss the ground when prostrating before a superior; to *worship*, ready "to fall down/prostrate oneself to adore on one's knees" (*DNTT*); to "do obeisance" (*BAGD*).
- ["The basic meaning of 4352 (*proskynéō*), in the opinion of most scholars, is to *kiss*… On Egyptian reliefs worshipers are represented with outstretched hand throwing a kiss to (*pros-*) the deity" (*DNTT*, 2, 875,876).
- 4352 (*proskyneō*) has been (metaphorically) described as "the kissing-ground" between believers (the Bride) and Christ (the heavenly Bridegroom). While this is true, 4352 (*proskynéō*) suggests the willingness to make all necessary physical *gestures of obeisance*.]

— Strong's Concordance
(Quoted from biblehub.com)

WORSHIP
(FROM THE HEBREW)

shachah: to bow down

- Original Word: שָׁחָה
- Part of Speech: Verb

- Transliteration: shachah
- Phonetic Spelling: (shaw-khaw')
- Definition: to bow down

Strong's Exhaustive Concordance
- bow self down, crouch, fall down flat, humbly beseech, do reverence, worship
- A primitive root; to depress, i.e. Prostrate (especially reflexive, in homage to royalty or God) — bow (self) down, crouch, fall down (flat), humbly beseech, do (make) obeisance, do reverence, make to stoop, worship.

— Strong's Concordance
(Quoted from biblehub.com)

¹ O come, let us sing unto the LORD: let us make a joyful noise to the rock of our salvation. ² Let us come before his presence with thanksgiving, and make a joyful noise unto him with psalms. ³ For the LORD is a great God, and a great King above all gods. ⁴ In his hand are the deep places of the earth: the strength of the hills is his also. ⁵ The sea is his, and he made it: and his hands formed the dry land. ⁶ O come, let us worship and bow down: let us kneel before the LORD our maker.

— Psalms 95:1 – 6 (KJV)

This passage is a great starting place to explore the true nature of worship. Verse 2 reveals a mystery of worship, as this psalm discusses coming into the presence of the Almighty. For these are the basics of what is really meant by worship. We are to prepare ourselves for His presence with singing and joyful noises. We are to make the journey into His presence with thanksgiving and Psalms. But as verse 6 instructs us we are to worship and bow down when we actually arrive in His presence. In most modern cultures we have lost the significance of bowing down.

In the times of the Bible, bowing was a significant action of adoration, respect, and submission. When a noble such as a knight or a prince bowed in respect to their king, they were indicating their loyalty and willingness to commit their resources to the king's direction. Bowing was, and is, an acknowledgement of superiority and/or sovereignty.

Nobles were men of great power, wealth, and armies of soldiers at their disposal. So, this bowing illustrated their commitment of all they had to serve the king's commands. This action without any words spoken signified to the king the nobleman was committing all he had, including his very life to the direction or command of the king. Take into consideration the definitions provided earlier and it's in this light where worship has its greatest significance.

So, as we come into the presence of God Almighty, worship is our attitude of respect, adoration, and complete surrender. It's neither what we say nor the songs we sing which demonstrates our worship, but rather the attitude we bring to Him. We can only come into His presence when our hearts offer all we are, and all we have to His will and control.

This is where worship becomes comparable to modeled behavior. As we submit to His Lordship over our lives and spend time in His presence, we learn who He is on a personal level. We gain an insight into His personality, His sense of humor, His attitudes, and characteristics. Worship brings us into the presence of God; His presence reveals His nature and character; we as His children then imitate Him.

He then becomes the ultimate source of behavior for us to model our lives into His image. Just as children duplicate the modeled behavior of their parents into their own personalities, so when we honestly and wholeheartedly enter into true worship we will imitate our Heavenly Father. It only stands to reason the more we worship the more like Him we become.

With the understanding of worship is our attitude of adoration, respect, reverence, and submission, let's look at how worship can be expressed. Giving physical expression to those attitudes is the mystery we are about to unravel. Outward demonstrations of worship can take any one of many forms. Let's look at some of the most common.

> *[9] He brought us here and gave us this rich and fertile land. [10] So now I bring to the LORD the first part of the harvest that he has given me.' "Then set the basket down in the LORD's presence and worship there. [11] Be grateful for the good things that the LORD your God has given you and your family; and let the Levites and the foreigners who live among you join in the celebration.*
>
> — Deuteronomy 26:9 – 11 (GNT)

We worship God by bringing our best to Him. In this passage, we learn to worship God by offering Him the first portion of our finances. This means we don't just give of the extra, but we separate God's portion first and then adjust our spending accordingly. This action signifies greater than almost any other we are truly and wholly dedicated to our Heaven Father. As Jesus put it,

> *For where your treasure is, there your heart will be also.*
>
> — Luke 12:34 (KJV)

True worship only begins with complete surrender, including our finances. God blesses our submission, more on this later.

> [1] *Praise God with shouts of joy, all people!* [2] *Sing to the glory of his name; offer him glorious praise!* [3] *Say to God, "How wonderful are the things you do! Your power is so great that your enemies bow down in fear before you.* [4] *Everyone on earth worships you; they sing praises to you, they sing praises to your name."* [5] *Come and see what God has done, his wonderful acts among people.*
>
> — Psalms 66:1 – 5 (GNT)

Remember praise is an expression of worship, in this passage worship is expressed as joyful shouts exalting God much like fans at a sporting event. Jubilantly singing in support of their favorite athlete/team; or the crowds excited bellows of joy at officiates ruling in their team's favor. Why should worship of the Creator of All Things be any less than the accolades bestowed at this type of event?

King David the Psalmist instructs us to be energetic in worship. We worship with our hearts fully engaged in His glorious presence. For, when we truly understand and appropriately value what it means to have an audience with our King of kings and Lord of lords we should not be able to contain our excitement.

Some scholars believe this psalm was written as a result of the Ark of the Covenant returning to the City of David. The Ark was the most sacred piece of Tabernacle furniture. The Ark represented the very presence of God and as such also symbolized the greatest victories won by God's people.

This Ark was once stolen by a heathen nation while under the protection of King Saul. As a result, this most treasured and holy article had for many years been separated from its proper place in the tabernacle. So, when King David brought it back and restored it to its place of prominence, all the people rejoiced with great shouts of joy and wholehearted voices lifted in praise. This was such an inspirational event even the King danced with "all his might." In fact, he danced in such an outlandish manner to embarrass his wife causing her to ridicule and despise him.

This picture sounds very similar to the thunderous excitement of fans at a championship event; much like a parade for champions. And why shouldn't our worship of the Almighty God be even more emotional than any display for an earthly accomplishment? Let's look at yet another psalm which supports this type of worship.

> ¹ *Hallelujah! Sing a new song to the LORD. Sing his praise in the assembly of godly people.* ² *Let Israel find joy in their creator. Let the people of Zion rejoice over their king.* ³ *Let them praise his name with dancing. Let them make music to him with tambourines and lyres,* ⁴ *because the LORD takes pleasure in his people. He crowns those who are oppressed with victory.* ⁵ *Let godly people triumph in glory. Let them sing for joy on their beds.*
>
> — Psalms 149:1 – 5 (GW)

Here we are told to worship with dancing; and to make music with the lively tambourine. Tambourines are lively; they cannot be played in a somber manner. The tambourine is a loud and fast paced instrument, which are not played during soft melodic musical numbers. Surely, we all have at least been around an ardent fan when their team or player makes a big play, and they jump up in some sort of victory dance. Perhaps you have also experienced a devotee of some musical entertainer, whose fans scream the lyrics to their favorite tunes while dancing until completely out of breath with sweat pouring out of every pore. The Psalmist here is describing this sort of behavior as a form of worship.

> ¹ *By David. I will give thanks to you with all my heart. I will make music to praise you in front of the false gods.* ² *I will bow toward your holy temple. I will give thanks to your name because of your mercy and truth. You have made your name and your promise greater than everything.* ³ *When I called, you*

answered me. You made me bold by strengthening my soul.

— Psalms 138:1 – 3 (GW)

This psalm teaches the worship of God is independent of location. David proclaims his determination to lift up praise in the presence of other gods as well as in God's house. It is important to have the attitude of determination to praise and worship God even in the places where it is uncomfortable, discouraged, or even prohibited. He is pronouncing his dedication to worship at any cost. For it when we worship in this manner, we can see His miraculous presence manifested.

Often political voices tell us to avoid actions which make others uneasy, but God desires us to love Him enough to declare our worship anywhere and everywhere! We reach the pinnacle of worship when we willingly risk it all for His glory, for worship is the attitude of surrender and allegiance to the nature and presence of God where we learn to imitate His divine character.

God says, "Be still and know that I am God.
I will be praised in all the nations;
I will be praised throughout the earth."

— Psalms 46:10 (NCV)

This verse would seem to contradict the notion of worship being loud and boisterous. As stated previously there are several expressions produced from an attitude of worship. And certainly exuberant and wholehearted praise is one such expression; however, it is not the only method of worship. We will now examine some softer examples of experiencing God's presence.

> [26] *Their ships were tossed to the heavens*
> *and plunged again to the depths;*
> *the sailors cringed in terror.*
> [27] *They reeled and staggered like drunkards*
> *and were at their wits' end.*
> [28] *"Lord, help!" they cried in their trouble,*
> *and he saved them from their distress.*
> [29] *He calmed the storm to a whisper*
> *and stilled the waves.*
> [30] *What a blessing was that stillness*
> *as he brought them safely into harbor!*
>
> — Psalms 107:26 – 30 (NLT)

Psalms 107 shows us God's presence can bring calm and quietness in the midst of our tumultuous lives. Worship, defined as experiencing God's presence through surrender and allegiance, is clearly demonstrated in this passage. When we are at our wit's end, staggering like a drunken man from stress we can seek the Lord and His presence brings a calm and quiet sense of safety. So, worship is not always loud and exuberant; sometimes it is in stillness we can experience the greatness of our God. The thing here is to remember to call on God in our troubles rather than attempting to solve them by ourselves.

> [11] *"Go out and stand before me on the mountain," the*
> *Lord told him. And as Elijah stood there the Lord*

> *passed by, and a mighty windstorm hit the mountain; it was such a terrible blast that the rocks were torn loose, but the Lord was not in the wind. After the wind, there was an earthquake, but the Lord was not in the earthquake.* ¹² *And after the earthquake, there was a fire, but the Lord was not in the fire. And after the fire, there was the sound of a gentle whisper.*
> ¹³ *When Elijah heard it, he wrapped his face in his scarf and went out and stood at the entrance of the cave.*
> *And a voice said, "Why are you here, Elijah?"*
>
> — 1 Kings 19:11 – 13 (TLB)

Elijah learned God's presence does not always appear in an extravagant fashion. Elijah was one of the greatest prophets during the days and times of the Old Testament; just prior to these verses He had defeated four hundred prophets of the false god Baal. In doing so, he angered the queen who favored this false god and she declared a death warrant on Elijah. He was now running for his life. In this story, he is isolated deep in a wilderness cave, hiding from his enemies, but God spoke to him and gave him instructions. It is often in situations like this where God's presence is revealed. Once again, He will prove Himself by gently and softly speaking to our hearts in times of solitude and meditation.

One of the clearest examples of worship demonstrated by experiencing God's presence through an attitude of surrender and allegiance, is found in the book of Joshua. For those who are unfamiliar with Joshua's story, he took over the leadership of God's people after the death of Moses. Moses led the people out of slavery and formed a massive nomadic nation, several million strong. During his time as leader God had performed many miracles, signs, and wonders—all to show Moses was His choice as their unquestioned ruler.

Joshua took over having spent more than forty years under the guidance of Moses. He knew Moses heard from God and he knew Moses had several direct encounters with God personally. As we begin our discussion of Joshua, he is on the verge of going into battle for the first time as this nation's leader. God had spoken to Joshua, but up to this point, Joshua had not had an encounter with God's physical presence.

> [13] *While Joshua was near Jericho, he suddenly saw a man standing in front of him, holding a sword. Joshua went up to him and asked, "Are you one of our soldiers, or an enemy?"* [14] *"Neither," the man answered. "I am here as the commander of the* Lord's *army." Joshua threw himself on the ground in worship and said, "I am your servant, sir. What do you want me to do?"* [15] *And the commander of the* Lord's *army told him, "Take your sandals off; you are standing on holy ground." And Joshua did as he was told.*
>
> —Joshua 5:13 – 15 (GNT)

First, let me address the identity of this unnamed man. When angelic beings were sent as messengers to instruct people, they never allowed the recipient of the message to worship them. And this man told Joshua to remove his shoes because the very ground he was standing on was holy. There is only one other place in all of scripture where someone was instructed to take off their shoes due to a sacred presence. When Moses met God for the first time and God spoke to him out of the burning bush, he also was instructed to remove his shoes. Clearly, God chose to take human form to speak directly to Joshua. Let's examine Joshua's encounter.

Once Joshua became aware the person in front of him was God, he assumed the posture of worship by bowing himself quickly to the ground. It's important to notice the first words out of Joshua's mouth, "I am your servant, sir. What do you want me to do?"

Joshua encountered the very presence of God Almighty and instantly knew his response must demonstrate surrender and allegiance. The first part of Joshua's statement "I am your servant" portrays his surrender or servitude. The second portion of his statement, "What do you want me to do?" illustrates Joshua commitment and allegiance.

From this text it is easy to make the connection between modeled behavior and worship. As we experience the presence of God through surrender and allegiance, we become acquainted with Him on a personal level. As we listen to His instructions and comply completely with His plans, purposes, and provisions we replicate Him and become like little children, just as Jesus commanded us in Matthew 18:3.

We have explored several examples in the Old Testament of worship. Now let's turn our attention to the New Testament to investigate any differences the sacrifice of Christ made on worship.

In the upcoming passage, Jesus is talking to a Samaritan woman, to whom He is in the process of revealing Himself as the Messiah, the Christ. She has been discussing the difference between the Samaritan and Jewish religious practices. Jesus is telling her neither set of observances will be accurate in the near future. Let's see what Jesus teaches about worship.

> ²³ *The time is coming when the true worshipers will worship the Father in spirit and truth, and that time is here already. You see, the Father too is actively seeking such people to worship him.* ²⁴ *God is spirit, and those who worship him must worship in spirit and truth."*
>
> — John 4:23 – 24 (NCV)

Jesus tells us we must worship God in spirit and in truth. What does He mean by this expression? We will dissect His statement to gain a fuller and richer understanding of worshipping God according to the New Testament.

What is worshipping in truth? Jesus declares, "God's word is truth" in chapter 17 and verse 17 of John's gospel. So, in light of this, worshipping in truth means to worship by appropriately applying the Bible; or, in other words, to worship God with our full understanding.

Jesus instructed us to worship in spirit. To fully understand this expression of worship we need to investigate 1 Corinthians 14. The entire chapter is integral for understanding context and integrity. However, the following selection is the pivotal key to unlocking the message.

> ¹⁴ *For if I pray in an unknown tongue, my spirit prays, but my understanding is unfruitful.* ¹⁵ *What is it then? I will pray with the spirit, and I will pray*

> with the understanding. I will sing with the spirit,
> and I will sing with the understanding.
>
> — 1 Corinthians 14:14 & 15 (MEV)

As illustrated by the Apostle Paul, we glean another way to worship which exceeds our education, training, or understanding. The entire 14th chapter of 1 Corinthians is devoted to the appropriate manifestations of the gift of "unknown tongues," both in the corporate worship setting as well as private worship.

As pointed out in verse 14, when we pray in another tongue our "spirit prays" in other words, we are praying to God in a manner which speaks to Him—spirit to spirit—bypassing our minds! Sometimes our minds are filled with thoughts which are at odds with God's plans and purposes, but when we allow the Holy Spirit to pray through our spirit we pray the perfect will of God. We can see this a bit more readily in Romans 8:26 & 27:

> [26] *In the same way the Spirit also comes to help us, weak as we are. For we do not know how we ought to pray; the Spirit himself pleads with God for us in groans that words cannot express.* [27] *And God, who sees into our hearts, knows what the thought of the Spirit is; because the Spirit pleads with God on behalf of his people and in accordance with his will.* (GNT)

Chapter 14 of 1 Corinthians makes a very clear distinction between public and private worship. Some things are most effective in private, while others are in public. As wondrous and awesome as this supernatural manifestation of the Holy

Spirit is there are certainly times when praying in tongues is ineffective and inappropriate; the corporate worship service for example. Paul the Apostle gives us very specific instructions on public demonstrations; look at the following verses from this same chapter:

> [2] *But if your gift is that of being able to "speak in tongues," that is, to speak in languages you haven't learned, you will be talking to God but not to others, since they won't be able to understand you. You will be speaking by the power of the Spirit, but it will all be a secret.*
>
> [18] *I thank God that I "speak in tongues" privately more than any of the rest of you.* [19] *But in public worship I would much rather speak five words that people can understand and be helped by than ten thousand words while "speaking in tongues" in an unknown language.*
>
> [23] *Even so, if an unsaved person, or someone who doesn't have these gifts, comes to church and hears you all talking in other languages, he is likely to think you are crazy.* [24] *But if you prophesy, preaching God's Word, even though such preaching is mostly for believers, and an unsaved person or a new Christian comes in who does not understand about these things, all these sermons will convince him of the fact that he is a sinner, and his conscience will be pricked by everything he hears.* [25] *As he listens, his secret thoughts will be laid bare, and he will fall down on his knees and*

worship God, declaring that God is really there among you.

²⁶ Well, my brothers, let's add up what I am saying. When you meet together some will sing, another will teach, or tell some special information God has given him, or speak in an unknown language, or tell what someone else is saying who is speaking in the unknown language, but everything that is done must be useful to all, and build them up in the Lord. ²⁷ No more than two or three should speak in an unknown language, and they must speak one at a time, and someone must be ready to interpret what they are saying. ²⁸ But if no one is present who can interpret, they must not speak out loud. They must talk silently to themselves and to God in the unknown language but not publicly.

— Romans 8:2, 18 – 19, 23 – 25, and 26 – 28 (TLB)

The word of God makes it very clear the Holy Spirit will cause neither confusion nor division among fellow believers. It is also abundantly clear God does not want unbelievers to be repelled by our actions, but rather convicted of their sin and drawn to forgiveness and redemption through Christ. We see Jesus promises this ministry of the Holy Spirit in John 16:7 & 8:

⁷ But I tell you the truth, it is better for you that I go away. When I go away, I will send the Helper to you. If I do not go away, the Helper will not come.

> [8] *When the Helper comes, he will prove to the people of the world the truth about sin, about being right with God, and about judgment.* (NCV)

Correspondingly, the Bible does proclaim public demonstrations have an appropriate setting as well; as we see in 1 Corinthians 14:26 – 27.

Public manifestations of the gift of tongues have some conditions to meet.

1. They must not confuse nor repel the unlearned and the unbeliever.
2. They must be followed by the gift of interpretation.
3. They can and will bring conviction of sin and draw the unbeliever into a relationship with Christ.
4. They are to follow a protocol of order based on mutual respect and common courtesy.

As a comment from my personal observation, meetings of five hundred or more people very often do not see the gift of tongues in operation due to the biblical criteria listed above. However, all the other gifts of the Holy Spirit can and should be in operation in meetings regardless the number of attendees. In his writing in 1 Corinthians chapter 14, the Apostle Paul's instruction on the gift of tongues does have a different set of guidelines than all the other gifts.

As a side note, the gift of interpretation is also a supernatural gift not to be confused with natural interpretation which is due to learning a language. These gifts of the spirit are listed in 1 Corinthians 12:8 – 10. All of these gifts are supernaturally given by the Spirit of God and are not based on our training, education, or even our understanding.

> [1] *While Apollos was in Corinth, Paul traveled across the hill country to Ephesus, where he met some of the Lord's followers.* [2] *He asked them, "When you put your faith in Jesus, were you given the Holy Spirit?"*
>
> *"No!" they answered. "We have never even heard of the Holy Spirit."*
>
> [3] *"Then why were you baptized?" Paul asked.*
>
> *They answered, "Because of what John taught."*
>
> [4] *Paul replied, "John baptized people so they would turn to God. But he also told them someone else was coming, and they should put their faith in him. Jesus is the one that John was talking about."* [5] *After the people heard Paul say this, they were baptized in the name of the Lord Jesus.* [6] *Then Paul placed his hands on them. The Holy Spirit was given to them, and they spoke unknown languages and prophesied.*
>
> — Acts 19:1 – 6 (CEV)

From this passage there are three major points we need to see:

- First, the gift of tongues is **not** required for salvation.
- Second, receiving the gifts of the Spirit is separate from accepting the gift of salvation.

- Thirdly, the gift can be received by the laying on of hands. We will look at other methods to receive this gift a little later in this chapter.

Paul the Apostle in verse 2 asks these people, which he had already identified as disciples, if they received the gift of the Holy Spirit simultaneously with salvation. As further proof, in verse 4 he identified they had been baptized in water with the baptism of repentance. This clearly shows the gifts of the Holy Spirit are in addition to the function of the Holy Spirit living in us when we accept Christ as Savior and Lord. So, salvation without receiving these gifts is clearly possible, however these gifts can be received concurrently.

Now let's look at the methods given in scripture for receiving the gifts of the Spirit. In Acts 10:43 – 47, we learn we can receive the gift of tongues simply by hearing the word of God preached.

> [43] *All the prophets spoke about him, saying that all who believe in him will have their sins forgiven through the power of his name."* [44] *While Peter was still speaking, the Holy Spirit came down on all those who were listening to his message.* [45] *The Jewish believers who had come from Joppa with Peter were amazed that God had poured out his gift of the Holy Spirit on the Gentiles also.* [46] *For they heard them speaking in strange tongues and praising God's greatness. Peter spoke up:* [47] *"These people have received the*

> *Holy Spirit, just as we also did. Can anyone, then, stop them from being baptized with water?"*
>
> — Acts 10:43 – 47 (GNT)

In this passage, we see those who were already believers identified the gift of the Holy Spirit because they heard these new believers speaking in new tongues. And from these scriptures we can see water baptism is not a prerequisite for the gift of tongues.

In this example, we are looking at the first encounter of the gospel being preached to Gentiles (those who are not Jews). So, the gift of tongues was definitely not just for the Apostles and those who had seen Christ personally, as some might teach.

In the next illustration we will look at the initial outpouring of the Holy Spirit, which was on a group of believers who were Jewish followers of Christ during His earthly ministry.

> [1] *Seven weeks had gone by since Jesus' death and resurrection, and the Day of Pentecost had now arrived. As the believers met together that day,* [2] *suddenly there was a sound like the roaring of a mighty windstorm in the skies above them and it filled the house where they were meeting.* [3] *Then, what looked like flames or tongues of fire appeared and settled on their heads.* [4] *And everyone present was filled with the Holy Spirit and began speaking in languages they didn't know, for the Holy Spirit gave them this ability.*
>
> — Acts 2:1 – 4 (TLB)

Here in this first encounter of man with the ministry of the Holy Spirit, a group of believers were praying (and most likely fasting) together seeking God for the comforter Jesus had promised to send in His absence. These were people who had already believed and accepted the Lordship of Christ, and when the Holy Spirit came upon them the visible expression of this gift was they spoke in languages not known by those speaking. So, the gift is also received by prayer.

> *Look, all of you are flawed in so many ways, yet in spite of all your faults, you know how to give good gifts to your children. How much more will your Father in heaven give the Holy Spirit to all who ask!*
>
> — Luke 11:13 (VOICE)

In these words of Jesus, He tells us the gift of the Holy Spirit is received by asking in faith. We know we need to ask in faith because James 1:5 – 7 says,

> *⁵ If any of you lacks wisdom, you should ask God, who gives generously to all without finding fault, and it will be given to you. ⁶ But when you ask, you must believe and not doubt, because the one who doubts is like a wave of the sea, blown and tossed by the wind. ⁷ That person should not expect to receive anything from the Lord.* (NIV)

If you would like to receive the gift of tongues; here is a sample prayer you can pray. Pray from the heart, and pray believing God will give you the gift of the Holy Spirit.

Heavenly Father, I ask for the gift of the Holy Spirit. I know according to your word it is your will to give me the gift of tongues. I want to pray and worship you beyond my human understanding. I ask in the mighty name of Jesus. Amen!

Tithe

PHYSICAL ACTIVITY

Every child needs opportunity and encouragement toward physical activity in order to develop muscle mass, coordination, and stamina. When children are denied access to physical exertion or are not encouraged to exercise often, in most cases they will suffer poor health both physically and mentally.

Tithing is the spiritual function which embodies the nurturing value of bodily exercise for us spiritually. For in tithing we honor and acknowledge God in a physical manner. Out of whatever we "do" to create an income we return the Lord's portion to Him. Whether we serve tables or own business entities which employs thousands; these physical activities generate financial resources for us which we must utilize to glorify our great and mighty God.

Tithing is **NOT** a difficult or painful task. I want to assure you there are huge, Huge, HUGE, **HUGE** advantages for us when we tithe. We will explore these tremendous blessings God bestows and promises to those who tithe. We will then look into the definition of tithe; we will examine the why of tithing; we will investigate the history of tithing, and we will search the scripture to understand how to appropriately tithe.

> [8] *"Will a man rob God? Surely not! And yet you have robbed me.*
>
> *"'What do you mean? When did we ever rob you?'*
>
> *"You have robbed me of the tithes and offerings due me. [9] And so the awesome curse of God is cursing you, for your whole nation has been robbing me. [10] Bring all the tithes into the storehouse so that there will be food enough in my Temple; if you do, I will open up the windows of heaven for you and pour out a blessing so great you won't have room enough to take it in!*
>
> *"Try it! Let me prove it to you! [11] Your crops will be large, for I will guard them from insects and plagues. Your grapes won't shrivel away before they ripen," says the Lord Almighty. [12] "And all nations will call you blessed, for you will be a land sparkling with happiness. These are the promises of the Lord Almighty.*
>
> — Malachi 3:8 – 12 (TLB)

Malachi chapter 3:8 – 12 will serve as the major foundational passage for our study of tithing, we will survey other scriptures, but we will regularly refer back to this passage.

To begin our exploration of the blessing of tithing let's look at verses 10 and 11. Verse 10 clearly proclaims we can test or "prove" God in this area of tithing. In essence, God is saying, if we don't believe Him, we should just try Him, and He will prove the benefits of tithing. He states He will open heaven and overwhelm us with blessings, so many; we will not be able to contain them. God's desire for each of us is to do well in life.

Matthew 7:11 says:

> ¹¹ *So if you sinful people know how to give good gifts to your children, how much more will your heavenly Father give good gifts to those who ask him.* (NLT)

This clearly tells us God is a far greater father than we could ever be, and He "will give good gifts."

Malachi 3:11 goes on to say God will protect us from the destroyer, our enemy. He further promises our efforts will be greatly productive. If we are not farmers, then our "field" is whatever we have chosen as our field of endeavor. If you are in the medical field, or the technology field, your vines are your areas of expertise or efforts. We have God's promise to bless and reward our efforts when they are surrendered to Him by tithing on the income.

These are amazing promises. God tells us to test Him, try Him, and prove Him. DARE TO TITHE AND WATCH WHAT GOD WILL DO IN YOUR FINANCES!

Let's now turn and look at the definition of tithe. We will look at both the Old Testament Hebrew and then the New Testament Greek word translated tithe.

First let's look at the Hebrew.

maaser or maasar or maasrah: tenth part, tithe

- Original Word: מַעֲשֵׂר
- Part of Speech: Noun Masculine
- Transliteration: maaser or maasar or maasrah
- Phonetic Spelling: (mah-as-ayr')

- Definition: tenth part, tithe

— Strong's Concordance
(Quoted from biblehub.com)

Twenty-seven of the thirty-two times this Hebrew word is used in the Bible, it is translated tithe. Its literal meaning is 1/10 or, in more common terms of today, 10%.

Now let's look at the New Testament Greek word for tithe.

apodekatoo: I take off a tenth part, pay tithe

- Original Word: ἀποδεκατόω
- Part of Speech: Verb
- Transliteration: apodekatoo
- Phonetic Spelling: (ap-od-ek-at-o'-o)
- Definition: to pay a tenth of
- Usage: I take off (deduct) a tenth part (of my property) (and give it away), pay tithe.

— Strong's Concordance
(Quoted from biblehub.com)

This Greek word is always translated as tithe. Clearly from both Greek and Hebrew tithe refers to 10%; which makes the math extremely simple. If you receive a paycheck, you just need to move the decimal over to the left by one digit then drop the last digit. Example $500.00 $50.00 so the tithe of $500.00 income is $50.00.

We have looked at the definitions for the word tithe; now let's turn our attention to the why of tithing.

Why would God care about our money? Isn't He just concerned about our heart and soul? Yes, He is truly and deeply concerned about our heart and soul. And this is exactly why He is very concerned about our money; Jesus said as recorded in both Matthew 6:21 and Luke 12:34:

For where your treasure is, there your heart will be also. (NKJV)

God desires and deserves our wholehearted love and devotion is indisputable. When we truly love we have no trouble spending money on the object of our affection's happiness. Remember in our discussion on worship we experience God's presence through surrender and allegiance. So then tithing is surrendering our finances to God's authority illustrating our true love and devotion to Him.

Reason number two (and most importantly) why we are to tithe is God, the creator of all things, proclaims the tithe as due Him. In fact, as Malachi 3:8 makes very plain, God considers withholding the tithe as robbery.

He desires to bless us more than we desire to be blessed, but if we take a stingy attitude we tie His hands. Because mankind is naturally sinful, all things human are by their nature cursed. Malachi 3:9 makes this cursed state of our finances very clear.

Now look very carefully at the wording of verse 9, it DOES NOT say God curses us for withholding the tithe, it DOES inform us we are cursed if we refuse to tithe. The source of the curse is from worldly money in our possession needing to be sanctified, purified, and dedicated to God for His blessing.

Without His blessing our money is a part of this world's system, which is under our enemy's (Satan's) jurisdiction. Our obedience with the first 10% makes the 90% blessed of God; 90% fully blessed of God will perform far better than 100% which is under the world's curse. To further explain this principle let's look at a teaching Jesus did on the issue of money.

> ⁹ *And Jesus went on to say, "And so I tell you: make friends for yourselves with worldly wealth, so that when it gives out, you will be welcomed in the eternal home.* ¹⁰ *Whoever is faithful in small matters will be faithful in large ones; whoever is dishonest in small matters will be dishonest in large ones.* ¹¹ *If, then, you have not been faithful in handling worldly wealth, how can you be trusted with true wealth?* ¹² *And if you have not been faithful with what belongs to someone else, who will give you what belongs to you?* ¹³ *"No servant can be the slave of two masters; such a slave will hate one and love the other or will be loyal to one and despise the other. You cannot serve both God and money.*
>
> — Luke 16: 9 – 13 (GNT)

Jesus illustrates mishandling money leads to distrust, which should not surprise anyone. How can we expect to be granted more if we are irresponsible with what we already have? In these words, from Christ's own lips, we see a demonstration of servitude. He reveals we have two choices: we either serve money living rebelliously toward God, or we serve God and faithfully rule over money.

Our Savior also alludes in this teaching faithfulness with money is rewarded with increases, which he also teaches in Matthew 25:21,

> [21] *'Well done, you good and faithful servant!' said his master. 'You have been faithful in managing small amounts, so I will put you in charge of large amounts. Come on in and share my happiness!'* (GNT)

To further illustrate God's claim to the tithe, let's examine a few scriptures; which will leave no doubt about His attitude regarding tithing. We must understand first and foremost we are His creation; all we are and all we posses already belong to Him.

As Psalms 24:1 declares,

> *The world and all that is in it belong to the LORD; the earth and all who live on it are his.* (GNT)

Without Him, there is no air to breathe, no water to drink; without Him, there are neither vegetables nor herbs to grow, no animals to breed for meat; without Him, we would not have skills to work, nor even exist at all. The tithe belongs to Him because it all belongs to Him and He claims the first tenth of our increases which He makes for us is holy unto Him.

To see this even more clearly, look at Leviticus 27:30 & 32:

> [30] *Ten percent of everything you harvest is holy and belongs to me, whether it grows in your fields or on your fruit trees.*

> [32] *When you count your flocks and herds, one out of ten of every newborn animal is holy and belongs to me...* (CEV)

A tithe, the first 10%, belongs to God simply because He claims it as His rightful and just due.

Tithing puts us in a financial covenant contract with God Almighty which places Him by His own promises in a position to guard our resources from destruction. This covenant does not entitle us to be irresponsible with those resources, but it does give us grounds to feel safe due to His care for our well-being. We have examined God's why for tithing; we now focus on the history of tithing.

Genesis 14:20 is the first record of tithing. This is where Abraham tithed to Melchizedek; he is known as the King of Salem and a priest of the Most High God. Nothing else is known about this man, and only one other time is he mentioned in the Old Testament which is in Psalms 110:4. This is a prophetic foretelling concerning the coming messiah, Jesus Christ, which we will examine more about this a little later.

Abraham is known to Jews and Christians alike as the father of faith. For with Abraham God makes the first covenant. Living approximately six hundred years before the birth of Moses, Abraham begins the tradition of tithing for him and his descendants, the Israelites.

God gives Moses the responsibility of recording the laws for the children of Israel during their travels in the wilderness. In the books of the law God gives fifteen specific instructions on tithing. There are at least twelve other verses of Old Testament scriptures which discusses the tithe, with the last of these occurring In Malachi (which we quoted in the opening of this section) nearly 1,000 years after God includes tithing in the law of Moses. So, in the Old Testament alone tithing is taught and confirmed throughout some 1,600 years of appropriately honoring God with our finances.

Now look at what Jesus says about tithing.

> *23 "What sorrow awaits you teachers of religious law and you Pharisees. Hypocrites! For you are careful to tithe even the tiniest income from your herb gardens, but you ignore the more important aspects of the law—justice, mercy, and faith. You should tithe, yes, but do not neglect the more important things. 24 Blind guides! You strain your water so you won't accidentally swallow a gnat, but you swallow a camel!*
>
> *25 "What sorrow awaits you teachers of religious law and you Pharisees. Hypocrites! For you are so careful to clean the outside of the cup and the dish, but inside you are filthy—full of greed and self-indulgence!*
>
> — Matthew 23:23 – 25 (NLT)

It should be apparent Christ is reprimanding the Pharisees for their attention to tithing on the minutia; all the while they are completely ignoring some very weighty character flaws. Jesus makes two points very clearly in this passage:

1. *Tithing neither excuses nor covers character flaws.* In other words, in the kingdom of God no one can buy their way along. Here's a warning from

the mind and lips of Christ to ministry leaders: just because a person has been successful in business does not necessarily make them a good candidate for positions of authority.
2. *Strength of character does not excuse us from tithing.* Appearing to have a strong moral character while omitting tithing is lopsided, because the driving force behind this behavior is selfishness. This is of course a major character flaw. Jesus makes it very clear both are to be done.

We have one more stop on this historical journey of investigation on tithing. The Apostle Paul writes about tithing in the book of Hebrews, some thirty years after the death of Christ.

Hebrews 7 is all about tithing and the New Testament church. During the era Moses's law, tithes were received by priests who were priests by birthright. During these times there were instances where priests of undesirable character received the tithes as their family heritage. After the death and resurrection of Christ, the Levitical priesthood is cancelled in favor of the eternal priesthood of Jesus Christ.

Paul tells us repeatedly in Hebrews 7:15, 17, and 21 Jesus is a priest in the order of an everlasting Melchizedek. And yet Melchizedek is only recorded in one place doing only one priestly duty, receiving the tithe from Abraham. So, Christ being an eternal Melchizedek means Jesus makes tithing an everlasting principle.

To this point we have explored the blessing on tithing, looked at the definition of tithing, examined the why of tithing, and investigated the history of tithing; now let's search the scriptures to understand how to tithe.

Paul instructs us to tithe to men in Hebrews 7:8,

> *Here mortal men receive tithes, but there he receives them, of whom it is witnessed that he lives.* (NKJV)

This scripture assures us when we tithe here in the physical realm; Jesus receives them in heaven where they are watched over eternally. We tithe to Christ, although in this realm they are received by men. This means we entrust Christ with our tithes, and release them into His charge, thereby we no longer have rights of control as to how those monies are spent. Ministers who receive tithes are responsible for the stewardship of those funds and will be judged by Christ for their actions.

To be biblically accurate in our tithing we need to follow the teaching in the word of God given in Malachi 3:10.

> *Bring all the tithes into the storehouse so that there will be food enough in my Temple; if you do, I will open up the windows of heaven for you and pour out a blessing so great you won't have room enough to take it in!* (TLB)

The storehouse is a metaphor representing the church, or God's house. By this we know the tithe belongs to the local church. And really this makes a lot of sense seeing it is the local church is our safe environment and the primary source of our spiritual provisions. Some may wonder about supporting other ministries or charities which is a good thing to do, however those monies are offerings over and above the tithe. Look at Malachi 3:8,

> *Will a man rob God? Yet you have robbed Me. But you say, In what have we robbed You? In the tithe and the offering!*

Again, it clearly differentiates between the tithe and the offering. In order to ensure a church is responsible and biblically accurate 10% of their gross revenue should be given to support other ministries such as missions and local food pantries. Biblical support for this test is found in Numbers 18:25 – 26,

> [25] *The Lord said to Moses,* [26] *"Speak to the Levites and tell them: 'You will receive a tenth of everything the Israelites make, which I will give to you. But you must give a tenth of that back to the Lord.* (NCV)

To be perfectly clear, just because our churches are tithing to support other ministries does not exempt us from giving offerings. When we are convicted in our souls by the Holy Spirit to support an additional charity we need to do so. However, it is an offering over and above the tithe which exclusively belongs to the local church.

We have seen tithes belong to the local church.

From the history of tithing, we gleaned a practice predating the Law of Moses by six hundred years and confirmed by the apostle Paul thirty years after Christ.

We tithe to show our devotion and obedience to God resulting in tremendous blessings for us when we tithe.

Share Christ with Others

UNCONDITIONAL LOVE

God loved the people of this world so much that he gave his only Son, so that everyone who has faith in him will have eternal life and never really die.

— John 3:16 (CEV)

[7] It is a difficult thing for someone to die for a righteous person. It may even be that someone might dare to die for a good person. [8] But God has shown us how much he loves us—it was while we were still sinners that Christ died for us!

— Romans 5:7 – 8 (GNT)

[12] My commandment is this: love one another, just as I love you. [13] The greatest love you can have for your friends is to give your life for them. [14] And you are my friends if you do what I command you.

— John 15:12 – 14 (GNT)

God has demonstrated in the most elaborate manner His love for us is total and unconditional. The above verses are just a few examples among many illustrating God's intensions toward us; however, true love is a two-way street—it is both given and received.

Unconditional love is the final element we will discuss in this examination of spiritual growth which parallels directly with sharing what Christ has done in your life with others. There is no question about God's unconditional love for us; the question is, "How do we illustrate unconditional love for Him?"

We need to explore the scriptures for what God desires from us. When we pray, praise, and worship we signify our desire for him. However, what He desires from us is more, much more. To get an idea of what Christ wants as an expression of our love for Him let's take a look at a portion of the last conversation Jesus has with Peter.

> [15] *They finished eating breakfast.*
> Jesus: *Simon, son of John, do you love Me more than these other things?*
> Simon Peter: *Yes, Lord. You know that I love You.*
> Jesus: *Take care of My lambs.*
>
> [16] *Jesus asked him a second time…*
>   Jesus: *Simon, son of John, do you love Me?*
>   Simon Peter: *Yes, Lord. You must surely know that I love You.*
>   Jesus: *Shepherd My sheep.*

> ¹⁷ *(for the third time) Simon, son of John, do you love Me?*
> Peter was hurt because He asked him the same question a third time, *"Do you love Me?"*
> Simon Peter: *Lord, You know everything! You know that I love You.*
> Jesus: *Look after My sheep.*
>
> — John 21:15 – 17 (VOICE)

Christ is using a metaphor in this discussion, because we have no record of Jesus owning a flock of sheep. This leaves us to question the reference to "His Sheep."

Some might portray His sheep as those who are following Him as their teacher. Others have proclaimed Christ was referring to the Jewish people, while many have claimed He was indicating the believers who soon coalesce into a global and everlasting church. However, God's word will enlighten us to a different definition of His sheep; let's look at Psalms 100:3 and Ezekiel 34:31.

> *Know that the Lord, He is God;*
> *It is He who has made us, and not we ourselves;*
> *We are His people and the sheep of His pasture.*
>
> — Psalms 100:3 (NKJV)

> *"You are My flock, the flock of My pasture; you are men, and I am your God," says the Lord God.*
>
> — Ezekiel 34: 31 (NKJV)

When we group these scriptures with John 3:16 (quoted earlier in this chapter) along with Psalms 24:1, which says,

> *The world and all that is in it belong to the Lord; the earth and all who live on it are his.* (GNT)

We see all the peoples of the earth are His sheep. To further illustrate this point let's examine a verse in 2 Peter.

> *The Lord is not slow to do what he has promised, as some think. Instead, he is patient with you, because he does not want anyone to be destroyed, but wants all to turn away from their sins.*
>
> — 2 Peter 3:9 (GNT)

In this verse, we see God desires all men to come to the saving knowledge of Jesus Christ. God the Father demonstrated His love for each of us by sending His Son to die, paying the penalty for each of our individual sins. We need to be keenly aware God would have sent Jesus to the cross if we were the only person saved by His sacrifice. He loves each of us that much! Because of His great love for us, we are saved from our own destructive natures. We are also spared the eternal torment of hell through accepting, by faith, Jesus Christ as our Savior. We do this by pledging our allegiance to Him as our unquestioned Lord and ruler of our lives.

God Almighty, the creator of the universe, has proven and given His unconditional love to us, and we show Him our unconditional love by feeding His sheep. We have examined what qualifies as His sheep. This leaves one unanswered question—what does it mean to "feed" His sheep?

If you remember from the discussion on reading and studying the Bible, we determined God's word is our spiritual nutrition, so in other words, it is our spiritual food. So, we feed His sheep by proclaiming the word of Christ to those He puts in our lives.

In John 14:15, Jesus also tells us we show our love for God by obedience to His commandments to love God and love one another as stated in John 13:34. In fact, according to the gospel of Mark 12:29 – 31, Christ states the greatest of all the Old Testament commandments are to love God with all our hearts, souls, minds, and strength, and then to love others as we love ourselves.

Paul exclaims, in Galatians 5:14 all the law is fulfilled by love. We are told in 1 John 4:7 – 12 the highest expression of love is to share the God who "is" love with those who don't know Him. As God's love enters our hearts, He empowers us and motivates us to love those around us!!

Read the following passages of scripture slowly and give them time to sink into your mind and your heart, and then read them over and over again, you will experience God's amazing love in a whole new way.

> *If you love Me, you will do what I say.*
>
> — John 14:15 (NLV)

> *I give you a new command: Love each other. You must love each other just as I loved you.*
>
> — John 13:34 (ERV)

All the Law says can be summed up in the command to love others as much as you love yourself.

— Galatians 5:14 (CEV)

²⁹ Jesus answered, "The most important one says: 'People of Israel, you have only one Lord and God. ³⁰ You must love him with all your heart, soul, mind, and strength.' ³¹ The second most important commandment says: 'Love others as much as you love yourself.' No other commandment is more important than these."

— Mark 12:29 – 31 (CEV)

⁷ Dear friends, we must love each other because love comes from God. Everyone who loves has been born from God and knows God. ⁸ The person who doesn't love doesn't know God, because God is love. ⁹ God has shown us his love by sending his only Son into the world so that we could have life through him. ¹⁰ This is love: not that we have loved God, but that he loved us and sent his Son to be the payment for our sins. ¹¹ Dear friends, if this is the way God loved us, we must also love each other. ¹² No one has ever seen God. If we love each other, God lives in us, and his love is perfected in us.

— 1 John 4:7 – 12 (GW)

Some may be concerned about what to say or even worried you might say the wrong things. DON'T BE AFRAID! Just tell them in your own words what a difference Christ has made in your life. None of us have trouble telling a friend or possibly a stranger about our favorite movie, sports team, or hobby. It really is simple! For convenience a simple outline of how to share Christ with others is included here.

HOW TO SHARE CHRIST WITH OTHERS

1. Men are sinners.

As the Scriptures say, "No one is righteous— not even one.

— Romans 3:10 (NLT)

For everyone has sinned; we all fall short of God's glorious standard.

— Romans 3:23 (NLT)

2. God is supremely holy; nothing impure, imperfect or tainted with sin will enter heaven.

Don't you realize that those who do wrong will not inherit the Kingdom of God?

— 1 Corinthians 6:9a (NLT)

3. Good works cannot produce eternal life.

> ⁸ *God saved you by his grace when you believed. And you can't take credit for this; it is a gift from God.* ⁹ *Salvation is not a reward for the good things we have done, so none of us can boast about it.*
>
> — Ephesians 2:8 – 9 (NLT)

4. This gift is received in three steps.

- a. Repent of sins.

> ¹⁸ *But God was fulfilling what all the prophets had foretold about the Messiah—that he must suffer these things.* ¹⁹ *Now repent of your sins and turn to God, so that your sins may be wiped away.*
>
> — Acts 3:18 – 19 (NLT)

> ¹⁹ *I correct and discipline everyone I love. So be diligent and turn from your indifference.*
> ²⁰ *"Look! I stand at the door and knock. If you hear my voice and open the door, I will come in, and we will share a meal together as friends.* ²¹ *Those who are victorious will sit with me on my throne, just as I was victorious and sat with my Father on his throne.*
>
> — Revelation 3:19 – 21 (NLT)

- b. Believe in your heart.

For this is how God loved the world: He gave his one and only Son, so that everyone who believes in him will not perish but have eternal life.

— John 3:16 (NLT)

- c. Profess Jesus Christ as your Lord.

⁹ If you openly declare that Jesus is Lord and believe in your heart that God raised him from the dead, you will be saved. ¹⁰ For it is by believing in your heart that you are made right with God, and it is by openly declaring your faith that you are saved.

— Romans 10:9 – 10 (NLT)

5. Explain a profession is more than mere words. A profession of faith is committing wholeheartedly to leadership of Jesus Christ. You are contracting with the God of the universe to live by His rules and submitting yourself to His divine will and purpose.
6. Pray a prayer like this in their own words and mean it with all their heart. They can repeat it after you.

Heavenly Father,

I come to you in the name of Jesus Christ; I confess I am a sinner. With Your help I will turn from all my sinful ways.

Father God, I believe Jesus is your miraculous son, born of virgin, and He died to pay the penalty for my sin, and You, the Almighty God, raised Him from the dead.

I declare from this day forward; Jesus Christ is my Lord. I surrender all I am and all I have to You.

I say to Satan and all his evil forces; you no longer have any control over me, because I belong to Jesus Christ completely and fully now leave in Jesus name.

I thank you, Father God, for the gift of everlasting life, and I receive it by faith in the name of Jesus Christ. Amen.

Final Thoughts

We have looked at what it takes to mature spiritually and compared it to our natural growth and development.

We have compared the safe environment of the family home to committed church attendance. This enables us to grow relationships with other believers, mirroring the peer interactions of physical development. Out of which we develop healthy social and emotional skills.

Daily Bible study was compared to proper nutrition, while prayer was our emotional support.

We saw worship is the means by which we experience the presence of God in order to imitate His character in the same manner we duplicate the behavior of our parents. We found tithing is the spiritual equivalence of physical exercise because it is honoring God with what we "do" for a living.

And lastly, we learned to both receive and give unconditional love for God by sharing Christ with others, which is how He showed His love to us as well as the whole world.

To further illustrate spiritual growth let's compare it to another common practice of recent times, of the internet and social networking.

In this example we make a decision to get online, which is like committing our lives to Christ (our spiritual birth).

Then we purchase an internet device and log onto the World Wide Web, which correlates to the safe environment of a local church.

Next, we explore different social networks and decide to join Facebook and connect with our friends, which is our peer interaction with other believers.

Then we login daily, and to read our messages, we check out our friends' posts. This is similar to reading our Bible for proper nutrition.

We notice Facebook has groups for people who want to communicate about a particular interest, say sports or photography. We join one and start chatting with others about those interests, which symbolizes the emotional support of prayer.

We enjoy these interactions to the point we decide to meet some of these people face to face and engage in and exchange tips on our common interests. This is the modeled behavior found in worship.

We discover one of these people shares more than a general interest with us, and we fall in love with them. Marriage is next, which is the committed physical activity of tithing.

We decide we want to have children with our spouse, which is the unconditional love which causes us to share the message of Christ.

In the natural world, all this happens over months or years. However, in the supernatural these are simultaneous.

In other words, from the first moment of our spiritual life in Christ we commit to a local church, fellowship with other believers, read our Bible, pray, worship, tithe, and share Christ with others all at once. We need to immediately incorporate all these growth factors into our daily life.

What is our lesson from this? Commit to a local church and go at every opportunity, fellowship with other believers everywhere we go and/or converse with fellow believers by phone daily if necessary.

We need to read our Bible, pray, and worship every day, just as importantly as eating.

Tithe on every income and share Christ with any and everyone.

These simple things are our joy and privilege in exchange for God's wonderfully amazing love and provision.

My prayer for you:

> *Heavenly Father,*
>
> *I pray for everyone who reads this book. I ask you to open their hearts and minds to hear your voice.*
>
> *I know your word does not and cannot be void of your power, so I trust you mighty God to surround them with your presence and overwhelm them with your amazing love.*
>
> *Teach them to let go of past hurts so they can forgive all those who have wronged them, and accept all the grace and purpose You, Almighty God, have for their life.*
>
> *Strengthen them by Your spirit Father to have the courage and confidence to step into Your throne room and declare their faith in Christ and trust in You.*
>
> *I ask these things in the glorious and all powerful name of Jesus Christ.*
>
> *Amen.*

Copyrights

Contemporary English Version (CEV) Copyright © 1995 by American Bible Society For more information about CEV, visit www.bibles.com and www.cev.bible.

English Standard Version (ESV) The Holy Bible, English Standard Version. ESV® Text Edition: 2016. Copyright © 2001 by Crossway Bibles, a publishing ministry of Good News Publishers.

GOD'S WORD Translation (GW) Copyright © 1995, 2003, 2013, 2014, 2019, 2020 by God's Word to the Nations Mission Society. All rights reserved.

Good News Translation (GNT) Good News Translation® (Today's English Version, Second Edition) © 1992 American Bible Society. All rights reserved. For more information about GNT, visit www.bibles.com and www.gnt.bible.

Holman Christian Standard Bible (HCSB) Copyright © 1999, 2000, 2002, 2003, 2009 by Holman Bible Publishers, Nashville Tennessee. All rights reserved.

Living Bible (TLB) The Living Bible copyright © 1971 by Tyndale House Foundation. Used by permission of Tyndale House Publishers Inc., Carol Stream, Illinois 60188. All rights reserved.

The Message (MSG) Copyright © 1993, 2002, 2018 by Eugene H. Peterson

Modern English Version (MEV) The Holy Bible, Modern English Version. Copyright © 2014 by Military Bible Association. Published and distributed by Charisma House.

New Century Version (NCV) The Holy Bible, New Century Version®. Copyright © 2005 by Thomas Nelson, Inc.

New King James Version (NKJV) Scripture taken from the New King James Version®. Copyright © 1982 by Thomas Nelson. Used by permission. All rights reserved.

New Life Version (NLV) Copyright © 1969, 2003 by Barbour Publishing, Inc.

New Living Translation (NLT) Holy Bible, New Living Translation, copyright © 1996, 2004, 2015 by Tyndale House Foundation. Used by permission of Tyndale House Publishers, Inc., Carol Stream, Illinois 60188. All rights reserved.

New Living Translation (NLT 1996) Scripture quotations marked (NLT1996) are taken from the Holy Bible, New Living Translation, copyright © 1996 by Tyndale House Foundation. Used by permission of Tyndale House Publishers, Inc. Wheaton, Illinois 60189. All rights reserved.

The Voice (VOICE) The Voice Bible Copyright © 2012 Thomas Nelson, Inc. The Voice™ translation © 2012 Ecclesia Bible Society All rights reserved.

Milton Keynes UK
Ingram Content Group UK Ltd.
UKHW020727110724
445228UK00013B/505